YOUR
BRAIN

Sally Hewitt

Quarto
Library

This library edition published in 2016 by Quarto Library.,
an imprint of QEB Publishing, Inc.

6 Orchard, Lake Forest, CA 92630

Distributed in the United States and Canada by
Lerner Publisher Services
241 First Avenue North
Minneapolis, MN 55401 U.S.A.
www.lernerbooks.com

A CIP record for the book is available from the Library
of Congress.

ISBN 978 1 60992 877 3

Printed in China

Publisher: Maxime Boucknooghe
Editorial Director: Victoria Garrard
Art Director: Miranda Snow
Series Editor: Claudia Martin
Series Designer: Bruce Marshall
Photographer: Michael Wicks
Illustrator: Chris Davidson
Consultant: Kristina Routh

Words in **bold** can be
found in the glossary
on page 22.

Contents

What does your brain do?

Your **brain** is inside your head. You think with this part of your body. Your brain controls everything you do. Even while you are asleep, your brain keeps on working.

▸Your dreams are what you are thinking about in your sleep.

Your brain tells your body to move. It tells you what you see, smell, hear, taste, and touch. It even tells you if you are happy or sad.

You learn new things and remember them using your brain.

Your amazing brain

Your brain is kept safe inside a strong box of bone called your **skull**. Your brain needs to be protected because it is soft.

Your skull is made up of two sets of bones. The bones of your face are in one set. The other set is just the right size and shape to cover your brain and is called the 'cranium'.

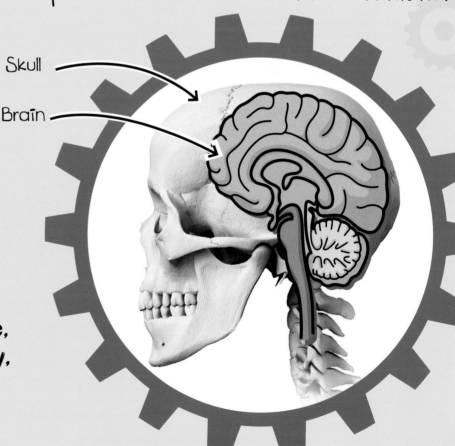

Skull

Brain

▲ Your brain looks like a wrinkly sponge, except that it's gray, not yellow!

Every part of your brain has a job to do.

You think with the biggest part of your brain.

The back of your brain controls how you move.

The brain stem makes sure your heart and breathing never stop, even when you sleep.

Nerves

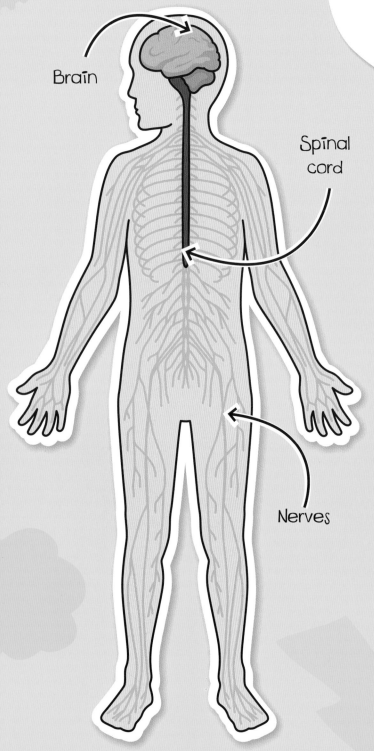

Brain

Spinal cord

Nerves

▲ Your spinal cord is joined to your brain.

Nerves carry messages from your brain to every part of your body and back again.

Your nerves are like pathways. Messages run up and down them.

Your spinal cord is a long bundle of nerves down the middle of your back. The nerves in your spinal cord link your brain to every part of your body.

Two kinds of messages are sent along your nerves. One kind goes to your brain to tell it what is happening. The second kind is sent by your brain to tell your body how to react.

This feels too cold!

Pull hands out of water until it warms up!

Activity

Feel something soft, such as the fur of a cat. A message tells your brain, "This feels soft!" Your brain sends a message back, telling your hand to stroke the cat!

Senses

Your **senses** tell you what is going on around you. You have five senses.

You *see* with your eyes.
You *hear* with your ears.
You *smell* with your nose.
You *taste* with your tongue.
You *feel* with your skin.

When you see something, a message is sent along your nerves from your eyes to your brain.

Apple!

Your brain tells you what you are seeing.

Your senses work together to tell you things.

Your eyes see flames, your nose smells smoke, your ears hear crackling, and your brain tells you: "Fire!"

Your skin feels hot and warns you: "Don't touch!"

Activity

Can you tell what something is by using only one sense?

Close your eyes. Smell an orange, soap, chocolate, and a flower. Which is which?

Now feel them as well. Does that help you to decide which is which?

Quick as a flash!

Some things you do so quickly, you don't think about them! If your finger touches a hot mug, you get the message "Hot!" and quickly pull your finger away. These are called 'reflex reactions'.

A flash of light makes you close your eyes tight. This is a reflex reaction. Closing your eyes protects them from very bright lights.

Are you good at hitting a ball? The more you practice, the faster your reactions will be. Your brain tells you instantly where the ball is going so you can hit it.

Activity

With a friend, drop a pencil between each other's hands. Can you catch it? Whose brain sends messages the fastest?

Memory

Your brain **remembers** things. When you taste new food for the first time, your brain records what it looks like, how it tastes and smells, and if you like it or not.

When you are given the food again, your brain can remember whether you liked it or not.

You can't remember everything, so your brain figures out what is important or not important. The more often you use a fact, the more likely you are to remember it.

What happened yesterday? Can you remember everything or just some important things?

Activity

Your brain is very good at remembering faces. Find pictures of ten faces. Show five of them quickly to a friend. Shuffle all ten faces together. Now spread them out. Can your friend remember which faces they have already seen?

15

Learning

When you do something new, such as learn to ride a bike, your brain and your nerves have to make a new pathway.

As you practice, messages keep going up and down the new pathway until you can ride really well!

Once you have learned how to ride a bike properly, you never forget how to do it.

Hard work and practice help you to learn new things, remember how to do them, and get better at doing them.

Activity

Try this. Write your name with the hand you don't usually use. Practice over and over again. Do you get better at writing with the "wrong" hand?

KIM   Kim
Kim

17

Feelings

How do you feel when you are invited to a party? How do you feel if someone borrows your favorite pen—then loses it? Do you feel excited, angry, sad, or happy?

You can usually tell how someone is feeling by the look on their face.

▸ Your feelings come from your brain.

Activity

Think of a feeling, then make your face and body show that feeling. Can your friends guess what the feeling is just by looking at you?

Feelings can come and go and they change all the time. Feelings can also help you to do the right thing at the right time.

If you feel afraid of a fierce animal, you keep away from it.

BEWARE OF THE DOG

If you feel happy to see your friend, you smile and your friend smiles back. You both feel happy and have a good time.

Healthy brain

There are lots of things you can do to keep your brain healthy.

Eat healthy food. Fruit, fish, vegetables, and milk are all good for your brain.

Keep your brain busy. Learn new things, play games, and do puzzles.

20

Chatting with friends and having fun is good for your brain.

Your brain does not need to work as hard when you are asleep, so get plenty of sleep and let it rest.

▲ Sport and exercise are good for your whole body, including your brain.

21

GLOSSARY

Brain

Your brain is inside your head. It is soft, gray and wrinkly, and it is the part of your body that controls everything you do.

Learn

When you learn, you discover something new and remember it. For example, you learn to read, or to ride a bike, and you learn new facts every day. When you learn something well, you become good at it.

Messages

Messages are facts and information sent from one place to another. Messages are sent along your nerves to your brain. If you see a bird, a message goes from your eyes to your brain. Your brain tells you: "Bird!"

Nerves

Your nerves are like pathways running from your brain to every part of your body. Messages are sent backward and forward along your nerves.

Remember

When you learn a new skill, you remember it. You don't forget it and you don't have to learn it again.

Senses

You have five senses—sight, touch, taste, smell, and hearing. They give your brain information about what is going on around you.

Skull

Your skull is the framework of bones in your head that protects your brain.

INDEX

NEXT STEPS

❋ Discuss how people are animals called humans. All animals have brains. Talk about ways in which other animals may communicate with each other. What noises do they make?

❋ Point to where your brain is. Talk about your skull, how it is hard and strong and the best shape to protect your brain. Look at the picture of the nervous system on page 8. Feel each other's spine and talk about how it is like a tube with the spinal cord running through the middle of it.

❋ Talk about how the brain lets us sense the world around us. You can point to the parts of the body you use to see, hear, taste, smell, and touch. Think of one thing you learn to do using each of your senses. What senses do you need to learn how to play the guitar?

❋ Play memory games together and exercise your brains. For example, say, "I went shopping and I bought some bread." The child repeats the item and adds a new one. "I went shopping and I bought some bread and some honey." Keep going and see how long your list can grow. The game stops when one of you forgets an item.

❋ Learn something new together, maybe a poem or a new activity such as juggling or a tune on the recorder. Talk about what you find hard and what you find easy when learning something new.

24